# STONE WITNESS

*a collection of poems by*

Richard Fleming

**BLUE
ORMER**

www.blueormer.co.uk

Copyright © Richard Fleming, 2017

ISBN 978-0-9928791-5-0

Published by Blue Ormer Publishing, 2017.

Cover image: *La Gran'mère du Chimquière*, courtesy of VisitGuernsey.
Photo of the author: courtesy of Jane Mosse.
Book layout and cover design by Stephen Foote.
Printed in Guernsey by Printed (www.printed.gg).

Richard Fleming has asserted his right under Section 77 of the Copyright,
Designs and Patents Act 1988 to be identified as the author of this work.

www.redhandwriter.blogspot.com

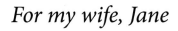

*For my wife, Jane*

# CONTENTS

# EDEN: THE SHORT VERSION

God gave Man
Paradise.
It all went
pear-shaped.

# FLOTSAM

*(noun: wreckage, remains, debris, detritus, waste, dross, refuse, scrap, trash, garbage, rubbish.)*

The sea does not want her.
It takes the others:
her, it discards
half-dead on shingle-sand,
the reek of salty fear
on brown skin.

Gulls shriek
and quarrel overhead.
She lies face down
barely breathing,
a human starfish,
one black asterisk
referencing nothing.

Cruciform
on wet shingle,
she counts her stations:
hunger, terror, flight,
abuse, exploitation,
a merciless sea
crossed.

Land
that does not want her
blurs like a mirage:
a half-moon cove,
gaunt trees
aligned like bars,
European houses.

She claws wet gravel,
draws herself
to her knees,
kneels to vomit.
Along the beach,
relentlessly,
policemen come.

# INVISIBLE

In the den, he hunkers down, holds his breath,
makes himself
invisible.

Oblivious, the Parkies stand six feet away
and speak in angry tones:
a broken pane, some daffodils beheaded.

He hears them toss his name
back and forth between them
and holds his breath to make himself invisible.

It is summer. He is eight years old.

He lies beneath white sheets and tries to breathe.
He is very small: not eight years old but eighty.
The room is full of snow.

Light spills through a high window
like radiance unfolding.

He hears voices rise and fall and makes himself
invisible.

The voices drift.
He hears them toss his name
back and forth between them
and tries to breathe.

What matter now, the broken pane, those headless daffodils?
Will summer come again?

He makes himself invisible.
It is easy now
with no more breath to hold.

# THE ARCHAEOLOGISTS

Digging again in Flanders Fields,
long trenches deep in red, rich earth,
that march in rows from east to west.

It rains. There is no shellfire now:
instead, with slow forensic skill,
they harvest artifacts from mud.

A pipeline has been promised: gas
to flow from here to Germany
but first, in one last push, they dig,

these archaeologists, who duck
beneath the trench's lip with spades
as once their forefathers, with guns,

crouched, cursed or wept, as shrapnel flew.
These modern men find badges, boots,
cups, broken rifles, helmets, more.

They work relentlessly in rain
to harvest relics from the soil
that runs like blood beneath their boots

while deeper yet, cold corpses lie:
bones, clothed in ragged uniforms,
reach from the weeping earth in vain.

# SUNDAY MORNINGS

Those Sunday mornings in her parents' bed,
tucked between them, tight,
she'd wriggle down, inhale their sweaty heat:
that smell, familiar, safe,
suffused with warmth and yet a salty, puzzling redolence.

They were her shelter: a cleft she grew in like an alpine flower.
Her father, red-cheeked, mountain-big,
made the bed tumble like a boat
when he yawned or stretched or turned;
while mother, plump and comfy, perched
at starboard edge, hand on the tiller, in control,

and she, snug and soft-nested between them,
was warmly content, secure in the moment, her future unspent.

# QUARRY

Pockets weighted with rocks,
she sinks like a stone, down
through engulfing blackness.
The sudden coldness shocks;
dark water spreads her dress
as she begins to drown.
Steep granite walls surround,
like hands, this black water:
their blunted fingertips,
coarse stone-scarred, cupped around
a pitchy ale. Her lips
imbibe it. Drowned daughter,
she descends through grey seams
hewn by generations
of quarrymen, long dead.
Her ears absorb the screams
of cutting-tools that fed
slabs to loading stations,
harsh shouts, profanities
and laughter, trapped in stone.
In bottomless darkness,
spinning, suspended, she
is free from time's duress,
constraints of blood and bone,
all that once assailed her.

Years will pass, rain and sure
forgetfulness will come
like longed-for sleep. Weeds will stir
her hair. She will become
timeless, unsullied, pure,
assimilated in
water, stone, and submit
her flesh to nature's game
then, snakelike, shed her skin,
while those that knew her name
will misremember it.

# HOUSE OF THE FAMOUS POET

*Listen to the caged bird sing:*
*such fine notes, yet oh so sad.*

A finch's soft throat spills,
like cut-flower blooms,
grace notes
in a narrow street,
where midday sun bleaches hung washing.

Old women's pachydermal faces stare,
black-shawled, from beaded doorways.
Cats sleep in corners, tails like question marks.
Switchblade-quick,
a lizard darts into a crevice
as sandalled feet trudge
uphill
towards a white citadel.

His house stands nearby,
one among many,
its green door in need of painting,
a lion's-head knocker,
tawny with rust.

I raise the iron ring,
rap twice
then wait and rap again.

The street is empty
but I feel observed.
Eyes watch beyond the beaded doors.

*Lì non ci abita nessuno!*
a voice calls out,
then silence gathers like fallen leaves.

I turn, retrace my steps.

Inside my head
a trapped bird
sings.

## NEXT PLEASE

No amount of perfume spraying
can reduce the underlying
scent of urine.
Does despair smell?
For that, too, pervades the day-room
where they sit, the old, the hopeless,
toothless, sightless, deaf, dumb, feeble,
staring, fearful, at the ceiling
or some mirage, in the corner,
no one else sees. The disorder
of their lives is like a puzzle:
pieces fail to fit together,
sky or trees or roof is missing.
There they sit and watch the seasons
come and go beyond the windows
and, on days considered clement,
some get out to sit on benches
or inspect the tidy borders.
Relatives come, fuss around them,
speak too loudly, move too quickly,
leave, dejected by the sadness
that pervades the rooms and spaces,
curtains, tiles, pale watercolours,
faded armchairs, plastic tables
and the pot-plants wilting slowly.

No one can pretend that hope lives
in these wizened, vacant faces:
rather, an alarmed awareness
that a dreadful thing approaches;
foul,
unthinkable,
misshapen;
something never meant to happen.

# CYCLE

The living world sails by, complete:
strange images engulf her; sounds
pour into her; she is caressed
by air, safe in the old bike seat
behind her father, the firm mounds
of his buttocks against her chest.

A young child, perched like a nestling,
in the metal-framed basket-seat:
his firstborn.  A small miracle,
the proud father thinks his offspring,
and to him, in the noisy street,
she clings, tight as a barnacle.

He pedals hard, pursued by time:
like roulette wheels, the bike-wheels whirl.
A breeze, around her soft hair, sings
with lyrical, unreasoned rhyme.
Euphoria engulfs the girl:
her arms reach out like stubby wings.

# TWENTY-ONE

We started out with cocoa tins
attached by string: a telephone
of sorts; progressed to proper phones,
old army surplus, wired them up
and strung a line from my bedroom,
to yours next door. We formed a link
that bound us fast through teenage years:
fifth form, sixth form, till, on you went
to uni, I to unsought work.
Where you were cerebral and gauche,
I was the opposite, and yet
we hit it off: no other friend,
before or since, meant half so much.
In those strange, final months, we seemed
to drift apart: you went away
and I, in turn, went somewhere too,
Estranged at twenty-one, we were.

You didn't live to twenty-two.

Your picture, pale, in newsprint grim,
beside the stark facts of your death,
remains my image of you now
a half a century away.
My vanished childhood friend, you look
so innocent, so fresh of face,
forever in a state of grace.

## LOVE IN HIGH PLACES

Hand over hand, upward we climb:
our leather sandals grip the wood
of an old ladder, each straight rung,
with confidence, as monkeys would.
In sunlit greenery, sublime,
above a canvas hammock slung,

we cling like two birds on a bough,
observing cricketers, white-clad,
a quarter-mile away, perhaps:
the batsman with his cricket-pad,
the running bowler bowling now.
We hear spectators' distant claps

but soon lose interest, for our love,
so selfish, all-consuming, new,
is all we need or want or feel,
and so ignore the humdrum view
of little lives we perch above,
for nothing but ourselves is real.

# CONTORTIONIST

Heels below chin,
a human ampersand,
she balances on slender hands
to watch the strongman boasting to three clowns
that he could bend an iron bar
to match the sort of complex knot
she twists her body into every day.

She knows it's nonsense: she alone
can warp her body, rubber-limbed,
to flabbergast a gawking crowd
and only then
by stretching hourly till the muscles ache.

A bull-necked braggart, she decides,
but handsome in an ugly way.
She locks her right foot
underneath her chin, sets her left free
and whispers: *Brute, untangle me.*

# THE MURCHEN QUARTET

## 1. RETURN

Midnight: a sickle moon, black trees in silhouette,
tall, jagged tops,
an electrocardiogram
scribbled on night sky.
Nearby,
a sloping meadow,
a derelict croft,
a dry-stone wall winding, like a serpent,
towards somewhere unseen.
Field-mice stir
in the emerald grasses,
a barn-owl hunts, soundlessly,
like a reaper's blade,
back and forth over dew-moist ground.
All is absolute, glistening stillness
hushed as the world's final breath.

He comes over the wall, rippling the darkness,
fluidly, spilling like water,
brown-booted, hooded, soft-footed,
moving with purpose and stealth,
crosses the meadow, head down-turned, hurrying,
curtained by camouflage, covert, concealed.

Kneeling, he opens a satchel,
secured by a leather-made leash
and gently releases,
as though giving birth,
two leverets, supple and sinewy-soft,
that huddle together, immobile as boulders,
to feel the soft night on their shimmering fur
and inhale the meadow, the moisture, the magic,
the coolness of grass, the moist sweetness of air.

Two young hares in the vastness of England,
two creatures dispatched to make Eden anew,
heed their ancestral summons and,
swallowed by darkness,
slip into the future, on cue.


2. DAWN

Each dawn,
the world, reborn, astounds:
sky, eggshell-blue,
grass greener, yet,
than far-off fields,
and mountains, a kaleidoscope
of purples.
Clear water, over polished rocks,
cascades
as wind unsettles trees.

Beside a zig-zag,
amber stream,
a dragonfly, with rainbow wings,
flicks like a fencer's blade.

Each dawn they view
their changed, unchanging world
fresh-made,
its energy,
its prehistoric, savage joy,
intoxicates them.
They flourish.


3. JOY

Awakened,
past erased, future
nonexistent,

their world begins afresh.

Only the extraordinary now,
a collision of senses,
exists.

Music.
Blackbird's flute,
grasshopper's fiddle,
drumbeat scuttle of field-mice,
accordion-wind in high meadows.

Silence.
In crystalline pools
trout glide like ghosts.
Owls, tombed in dead trees,
imitate death.
Dreamlike,
in the magical moment,

hares dance.


## 4. SURVIVAL

Stillness is her best defence.

So she becomes
a russet stone,
a dark tussock,
a clod of earth, upturned,

perhaps merely a shadow,
there, by a dry-stone wall
on hostile, open ground.

No shiver of wind
disturbs her tawny fur.

She sits, unbreathing,
stiff as an idol.

Only her eyes, bead bright
in a fine-boned head, travel
like planets.

With leather-gaitered boots,
mountainous shape,
tobacco reek,
and slow-departing tread,
danger passes.

# THIS BE THE OTHER VERSE

*In Memory of Philip Larkin 1922 -1985*

They carve in stone, engravers do,
Your name with start and finish dates
Then hand it to some cleric who
Abuses boys and masturbates,

Who then invites a bunch of craps
Up to the Abbey in best suits,
For lengthy speeches and back slaps,
Daft eulogies and organ toots.

It fucks you up, this being dead:
But I was fucked up long before.
I left behind so much unsaid
And, still unwritten, poems galore.

But now, turns up a stone that's like
A library book long overdue.
I sit on my celestial bike
And, gazing down, applaud the view.

# ORIGINAL SIN

Catechism came with porridge
on Sunday mornings, then.
Question
and Answer.
*What is man's chief end?*
A lifetime later, adult, grown,
I have the forthright answer still:
*To glorify our God, Amen.*

How those morning pictures linger.

With hair slicked down and parting straight,
scrubbed knees, nails free of grime, clean hands,
in Sunday Best, fresh underpants
and vest, black brogues with Bible shine,
I went with hymn-book to the church
then into Sunday School we trooped
like little soldiers off to war,
while parents stayed for Hell-Fire words
and promises of Satan's wrath
that they, in turn, would promise us.

Grey were the Sundays of my youth:
shut shops, shut faces, shuttered hearts.
A football kicked would damn to Hell.
A comic read, a careless laugh,
would be recorded in God's book.
Guilt was instilled and mortal fear.
I haven't yet got off the hook.

# LOVE STORY

*'Love is not love that alters when it alteration finds'*
*W. Shakespeare. Sonnet 116*

I thought myself in love. I lay awake
imagining your hair spread out like gold
and whilst asleep it glistened as I dreamed:
such lustrous tresses, how I loved to touch.
All changed the day you had your hair restyled ...

you came home shorn and while I wept you smiled.
I yearned for love but that was my mistake:

I never guessed love could turn quickly cold.
Love was a fantasy or so it seemed:
I loved you little, loved your hair too much.

I thought myself in love but I was wrong.
I loved you only when your hair was long.

# THE EXILE

*For Peter Kenny*

A taxi hurries through lanes
of green-banked-granite stillness,
its hunched driver taciturn, sullen,
solidly steering a wheel that turns
right then left in a vibrancy of air.
Suitcase on knees cradled,
his exile eyes see-saw
from London-grimed leather
to primrose banks at every turn.
Falling in love again, he marvels,
at salt in the wind, small cottages,
a tortoiseshell cat by a blue post-box,
at the lost Lilliputian scale of things
that once appeared
immense.

# MEN IN ICE

Three figures, shrouded by a broken tent,
lie, curled like commas, in icy death.
A group of living men
with breaths, collectively,
like exhaled ghosts,
pronounce for them
a brief but solemn prayer
and execute one last salute,
then leave departing footprints in fresh snow.

Years pass.
A century of change occurs.
Two great wars come.
God dies.
Prayers seem a waste of effort.
Man strives for planets not for poles.
Sons become fathers, grandfathers, then dust.
Scott, Bowers, Wilson, shrouded still,
lie frozen in Antarctica,
as far from home as any man can be.
Entombed in ice, preserved
unchanged, they seem to sleep.

Amongst the floating bergs
a massive silence rings.

# HIS MOTHER DANCES

Crouched on the stairs, he sees her dance:
her feet glide over lino squares,
with wireless playing sweet and low.
She waltzes, as though in a trance,
alone, amidst pans, table, chairs,
white kitchen sink, her eyes aglow.

Those slender arms grasp empty air:
her partner is invisible.
She circles, sweeps and murmurs words,
song lyrics or a lover's prayer.
What seems to him incredible
is how the music, like small birds,

whirls round his sleepy, tousled head
and makes him sad. The dancing stops.
His mother, hungry for romance,
settles for washing plates instead;
talks to herself, while he eavesdrops.
His father never liked to dance.

# IN GRACE

The present is arcane and strange
and any recollection left
of what has happened in the past
is vague and liable to change.
Of future plans, he is bereft,
for nothing now is hard and fast.

They give him multicoloured pens
and paper, as one might a child.
Familiar voices interweave.
He sees, through a distorting lens,
people who wept, people who smiled,
that, one by one, stood up to leave.

He is content. He lives in grace.
What matter if the moments blur,
if his nocturnal thoughts are grim?
He has escaped himself: his face,
a kind of absence in the mirror,
comforts and somehow pleases him.

# A POEM ABOUT LOVE

The ward is white and clinical:
tiles underfoot, strip-lights above.
The nurses kind but cynical.
This is a poem about love.

One moment all was well, then not,
and since that day, you have not stirred.
They say, have hope, but I cannot.
I speak your name: it goes unheard.

Young nurses come, young nurses fuss:
they check the tubes that give you air,
that wrap you like an octopus
as you lie sleeping, unaware.

This is a poem about love,
how love endures, how love survives
and how, when push turns into shove,
though strength has gone, more strength arrives.

Time stopped for us the dreadful day
you stopped, so now I too mark time
and try to keep despair at bay
with poetry and mumbled rhyme.

A tent of clear, enfolding mesh
cocoons you like a fine lace glove:
I cannot even touch your flesh.
This is a poem about love.

Immobile, comatose you lie,
a captured bird that yearns for flight.
We hang suspended, you and I
like sleepers between night and light.

# PICNIC

The first image
is always a tartan rug,
then, swiftly, other items follow:
Dad's parked Austin, monochrome,
Mum's picnic basket, acres of beach,
Atlantic breakers rolling in
and, there, behind my milk-white shape,
huge sand-dunes rising.

Splayed cricket-stumps swim into view,
a ragged bat, beach-ball and thermos flask,
Father in a deckchair, rolled trouser-legs
exposing freckled calves,
my brother with a bucket, spade,
constructing sandcastles and moats,
my sister with her rouge-faced dolls,
our mother counting sandwiches
while Laddie runs and barks at kites.

This is a poem I write and write,
failing, each time,
to capture those remembered hours.
They glide like feathered ghosts,
gull-shadows on a summer beach.
Mere words, inadequate,
spill from my clutching hands again.

## AWAKING ADAM

He wakes from dreams of emptiness and void,
a universe expanding, unimpaired,
and crystalline light that crashes over him
like a sparkling wave.
He sits up and the planet tilts: trees rush upward
into cloudless sky; mountains rearrange themselves
as rivers begin to flow.
Everywhere is birdsong and shimmering air.
The world invents itself, stone and substance:
he names its parts to give them credence.
His own shape, reflected in water, he calls Man.
Upright, spread feet in warm soil, he feels
earth's pulse drumming, light enfold him,
scent of leaf and blossom thrill his nostrils.
His eyes scan a roaring sky
where stars, invisible, await
his unexplored tomorrows.

## STONE WITNESS
*La Gran'mère du Chimquière*


Stone,
old, old stone, I groan with age.

Gran'mère, Earth Mother,
I stand sentry beyond the churchyard gate,
and watch, with sightless eyes,
the snail of human traffic creep along.

I am old and granite-cold: your island's anchor-stone.

Your fathers' fathers came to me
to pray, to lay or lift some minor curse:
an endless chain of island men,
one generation to another,
linked.

Four thousand years grown old I am. Imagine.

Still they come,
their mode of dress and manners changed,
their supplications much the same:
love, fertility, wealth, happiness, a long life free of pain.

Young children step tip-toe,
lay yellow garlands on my weathered brow,
or proffer coins that glitter in the sun.
They stand before me,
gaze up to my strange Earth Mother face,
and murmur spells as old as time itself.

Rooted here, I listen
as the salt breeze sings of breaking waves,
of fishing-boats and lobster-pots,
greenhouses, leafy water-lanes,
smart pillar-boxes, shining blue,
and amber cats asleep
on sun-warmed granite steps.

The soft breeze sings
of that so-lovely town
that climbs up to the sunlit summit of a golden hill,
the dauntless castle and the ragged rocks
where angry currents run.

Four thousand years grown old I am. Imagine.

Islanders, I anchor you.
Primeval, granite, I remain unchanged,
unchanged in a strange world of change.

This gemstone island, Guernsey,
this sea-locked rock whose timeless granite
birthed me,
whose good folk
shaped me,
this
my ancient magic will protect
and cause to prosper.

# OCTOBER RAIN

An aspen in a Norman wood
supplied the shaft.
A craftsman's patience
straightened, seasoned,
then perfected
something far removed from nature,
shaped the taper, sealed it,
gently carved the narrow nock.
Fingers, that might pluck a lute
on fair-days, set to fletching:
grey-goose feathers,
resin gum,
fine thread of linen.
These would aid trajectory,
ensure trueness of flight.
Lastly, a hand affixed with care
an arrowhead, the killing-piece,
fierce-furnace-forged
into a kind of bird-wing-shape
with pointed beak, as lethal as a battle-sword.

It would be one of many
that French archers took to English soil
to fly in flocks like starlings
over Hastings' fields
and fall to earth like iron rain,
out of a grey October sky,
to pierce the fearful blue of Harold's eye.

# RECLUSE

All scattered to the winds and ways,
like blushing cherry-blossom blown,
the friends, he knew when not full-grown,
have vanished from his elder days.
The carelessness of childhood meant
that friendships were a thing to find
then let escape. No contract signed.
No deal. A currency unspent.
If friendships had been coins or gold,
he might have locked inside a cage
all he had gathered to assuage
the loneliness of growing old.

# LAST MOMENTS

In these last moments, suddenly,
whatever hinges things breaks free.
A great wind blows throughout the world.
Dry riverbeds regenerate. Streams cascade.
Mountains shrug themselves awake. Growth accelerates.
Shoots burst through barren ground. New buds proliferate.
Saplings transform, in moments, to sky-beseeching trees.
Flowers paint drab valleys rainbow-bright.
Birds fall silent then, more sweetly, resume their song again.
Fish glide, like ghosts, through glacial pools.
In auburn earth, young foxes stir and wake. The agile hare
evades pursuing hounds.
A kestrel hovers like a tawny sword.
A field-mouse, made invisible, ascends a swaying stalk.
Hunter and hunted are reconciled.
Moor ponies, with apple-scented breath,
stamp restlessly and sniff the wind.
Cattle stand like statues. Sheep transmute to stone.
The grasshopper falls silent. The bee's refrain ceases.
The butterfly's wings open like a red fan.
Forests, darkly velvet, roar with blood and noise.
Deserts, measurelessly mean, mysteriously, become green.
In these last moments, timelessly,
whatever hinges things breaks free.
The earth trembles like a drum-skin.
Ancient boulders split like eggshells.
Wild children emerge
to gather flowers and prophesy.

# RED UMBRELLA

It rained.
You held a red umbrella high,
leaned into me and whispered,
*Sod the rain.*
I realised that something had begun
that was unstoppable.

Time's devoured
a lifetime of embraces since that day.
Now pain spreads like a red umbrella
as you lean into me.
The pillow, like an angel's wing,
kisses my bloodless lips.

# ICARUS

I am falling from high
but they do not notice.

The air, through wings
that promised much,
keens like a mourner.

Creeping ants below
evolve
to shepherd, ploughman, angler.

I fall unseen.

Someone
will dream it later.

I have no time
to scream.

The water is
hard as stone.

# IMAGES

This is a tree, he said and pointed to a tree.
We have seen images, they said.
There are many trees, he said. This tree is cedar.
We have seen images, they said.

Here is a flower, he said and pointed to a flower.
We have seen images, they said.
There are various flowers, he said. This is a rose.
We have seen images, they said.

This is a cat, he said. See it move. Watch it stretch.
Just like the images, they said.
This is a dog, he said. Watch as it wags its tail.
Images are better, they said.

That is the sky. Those small birds are swallows, he said.
We have seen images, they said.
Over there are blue mountains and a lake, he said.
Can we go back inside? they said.

# LAMENT

Ice petals on the blackthorn bough,
in twilight, masquerade as white
but it will never blossom now.
The world is slipping into night.
Weep for the last-extinguished light.

For generations to be born
into a world without birth-right,
for darkness, fast approaching, mourn.
Weep for the last-extinguished light.

Grieve for the final, breaking wave
that slips away, the bird in flight
that falls to earth, the hungry grave.
The world is slipping into night.

Tears in the grey, relentless rain
resemble signatures we write
on farewell notes imbued with pain.
Weep for the last-extinguished light.

Lament the sharpness of the blade,
the flesh, so vulnerable and slight,
the future plans so rashly made.
The world is slipping into night.

We cannot halt or abrogate
the bullet in its ghastly flight,
the torrent of extremist hate.
The world is slipping into night.
Weep for the last-extinguished light.

# TURQUOISE SKY

The child's eyes are full of fear. He sees
light subtly altered, fields pulsating red.
*Be a brave soldier*, his mother soothes
and tucks him back in bed.

His father's eyes are full of fear. He yells:
*Get ready Men*. Men tremble in the pit
then go over the top, following his shout.
Soldiers in dirty khaki kit.

No time for words or thoughts of home.
Only a moment to glance upwards and spy
something silver falling towards him
out of a turquoise sky.

# FUTURE AWAITS

It slips from an old diary, a monochrome,
foxed photograph. A couple, eighty years ago:
my parents, before parenthood,
in clothes that were the fashion then,
together pressed, bright eyes, dark hair,
and younger, younger than they ever were.

Could either have imagined then,
while posing for the camera, their faces pinked
by chill Atlantic wind, how swiftly life would hurry on
through marriage, childbirth, age and death?
How could they see themselves as part of history
when life itself was still a mystery?

Yet there they sit. Each one an integral part
of a long narrative that still scrolls by. I take
the story forward, pass it on. My siblings too,
our children, perpetuate the tale. The future waits
impassively. I marvel that with love alone
we brave the terrible unknown.

# JUDEN

*In memory of Irene Nemerovsky, murdered at Auschwitz 1942.*

Prodded, harried, without hope,
she gathered items in a case,
essentials that might see her through
this ordeal: spectacles, soap,
fresh underwear, a blouse or two,
a photo of a cherished face.

The books she wrote, to great acclaim,
would speak for her. She was resigned:
a helpless rabbit in a snare.
Her children, elsewhere, played a game,
all innocence and unaware.
Her door was left ajar behind.

Then hurriedly and under guard,
she trod in step with others who,
each with a fever-yellow star,
were herded to a station yard
to ride a fetid railway car
to Auschwitz in the morning dew.

## MEMENTO MORI

An ambulance howls like a hurt cat;
parts traffic as Moses did the waves.
Worms burrow in awaiting graves.
A police car buzzes like a gnat.

Stuck in a jam of steaming cars,
I contemplate how life transforms
in moments. How they wait, those worms,
so patiently, for us, for ours.

# KING OF THE HILL

Stone hand upthrown,
he faces west:
sharp-browed, stern-eyed,
tall, statuesque.

Read the inscription at his feet:
*A worthy man whose noble deeds
set him among the town's elite ...*
and yet, the epitaph misleads.

A robber-baron in his day,
then changed, by circumstance and luck,
to city elder, feet of clay
well hidden, so no thrown-mud stuck,
he ruled his little fiefdom well
and saw his enemies destroyed
without remorse. Who could foretell
that such a man, one so devoid
of gentleness, with traits like those,
would be immortalised in stone
and, in this hand-hewn granite pose,
transcend mere flesh and blood and bone
to stand now, haughty and austere
upon a lofty plinth that reads
*An honest man in every sphere ...*
*A worthy man whose noble deeds ...*

Such sentiments are seldom true:
all's foolishness, a massive bluff.
Man needs to forge idols anew:
mere gods alone are not enough.

# TITANIC

Stiff-collared and stiff-upper-lipped,
they bade their womenfolk go first,
with children, into lifeboats
that were only there for show,
then, ramrod-straight on tilting decks,
they braved the icy, ill-starred night
or went below to congregate
with other men, pale, poker-faced,
in state-rooms loud with jokes and boasts,
to camouflage their growing fear,
as cocktails, spilled, or scattered cards
made nonsense of forlorn attempts
at nonchalance.

In that dark realm of bitter cold,
of signal-flares and glacial stars,
where massively impassive bergs
moved sure and silently as gods;
where all around, like tombstones, ranged,
squat ice-flows gleamed a ghostly white,
snow fell, in feathered silence, then
on black waves breaking endlessly
on lifeboats, where survivors prayed,
their upturned faces, pinched and wan,
for fathers, lovers, husbands, sons;
but when such supplication failed,
prayed only for salvation.

# JIHAD

*In memory of Father Jaques Hamel, aged 84, who was murdered by Islamists while in Church at Saint-Etienne-du-Rouvray, France in 2016.*

The video shows backs and heads
of figures, blackly inexact:
once seen, the memory persists.
We watch an old man being hacked,
releasing blood that swiftly spreads,
by two young knifemen, *Jihadists*.

A priest, preparing to say Mass,
who should, one day, have died in bed:
a harmless man, no one of note,
who, on his knees, prayed as he bled.
*Forgive them, Heavenly Father*, as
they thrust him down to slit his throat.

# REQUIEM FOR A GAMBLER

All that you owned when at your peak,
with business buzzing like a hive,
was squandered on a losing streak
while, hopelessly, hope stayed alive.
No game of chance could you forgo:
you'd kiss the dice for one more throw.

Slow horses, greyhounds half asleep,
the Poker games you always lost,
the endless nights you got in deep
with fools who didn't count the cost,
the roulette wheel's capricious spin,
those gambles you could never win

left you like this: a rented room,
two threadbare suits, grease-stained and creased,
a stack of bills that I assume
no one will pay since you're deceased.
You always were an optimist.
Where are they now, those dice you kissed?

# ENDGAME

A lifetime of evasion, flight,
has ill-prepared me for the night
that fast approaches whilst I flee
with my poor harvest gathered in,
my talismans against the dark:
the holy book, the foolish grin,
the fearful, nonchalant remark,
I mutter, unbelievingly.

# APPENDIX

EDEN: THE SHORT VERSION: Like many ventures, this one started out well.

FLOTSAM: The refugee crisis in 2016 inspired this poem, which was runner-up in a UK poetry competition the same year.

INVISIBLE: As I grow older I become increasingly aware of how swift is the passage from childhood to old age and how, having achieved the latter state, memories of one's early years become ever more vivid.

THE ARCHAEOLOGISTS: How strange it must feel to excavate an area where First World War soldiers dug trenches just over a hundred years ago. The news report that prompted this poem claimed that archaeologists were working frantically to harvest war relics before construction teams moved in to lay a pipeline uniting Flanders with Germany.

SUNDAY MORNINGS: This poem, which received a commendation from former Poet Laureate, Sir Andrew Motion, was inspired by my wife Jane's childhood recollections of Sunday mornings, which, had I been aware of them when I was being marched off to Sunday School, would have made me envious.

QUARRY: In the Bordeaux area of Guernsey are a large number of disused, now water-filled quarries, a hangover from the days of granite extraction. I find them disturbing. Who knows what lies beneath the surface of these darkly sinister lakes?

HOUSE OF THE FAMOUS POET: I suppose this imaginary pilgrimage to the erstwhile home of an admired literary figure, Neruda perhaps, is ultimately a sad one. *Lì non ci abita nessuno!* translates as No one lives there!

NEXT PLEASE: My parents died in their early seventies so I have been spared the experience, common to many of my contemporaries, of visiting elderly family members in care homes. I expect that these places await all of us who live sufficiently long, but I can't say the prospect appeals.

CYCLE: I wrote this poem in Italy, having seen a young father cycling with his daughter on the pillion. Over forty years ago, in Scotland, I, too, often cycled with my own daughter perched behind me on a rickety old bicycle I'd bought from a junk-shop in Edinburgh.

TWENTY-ONE: My friend, John Simpson, died at the age of twenty-one in tragic circumstances. We experienced our unruly teenage years together. I suspect that, in later life, we never again manage to forge such heady and joyous friendships.

LOVE IN HIGH PLACES: First love is a breathtaking experience, a constant high, at least it was when I was young, and the lovers, who believe they have discovered an emotion no one else has ever experienced, have no interest in anyone but themselves.

CONTORTIONIST: As a child, the circus enthralled me and its array of amazing characters still manages to capture my imagination.

THE MURCHEN QUARTET: Murchen is Gaelic for Hare, a central character in Irish and European folklore. The hare is a truly beautiful creature that has long fascinated me. The four poems that make up this quartet are my homage to that enchanting beast.

THIS BE THE OTHER VERSE: The unveiling of a memorial stone for Philip Larkin was long overdue when it took place in 2016. I used Larkin's much-loved poem, This Be The Verse, as the template for this tribute to my favourite Twentieth-Century poet.

ORIGINAL SIN: Post-war Belfast was a grey place and never more grim than on a Sunday, with nothing to alleviate the dreary hours between church services, morning and evening, and the constant threat of punishment to any child that failed to treat the Sabbath Day with proper respect.

LOVE STORY: This lighthearted sonnet, the only formal poem in the collection, apart from the villanelle, Lament, was inspired by Shakespeare's lines from his Sonnet 116.

THE EXILE: My friend, the poet and playwright, Peter Kenny, grew up in Guernsey but was later whisked away to live in England. He still regards the island as his spiritual home and returns on a regular basis.

MEN IN ICE: In 1912 a search party found a tent containing the frozen bodies of Captain Scott, leader of the ill-fated Terra Nova expedition to the South Pole, and two members of his party, Wilson and Bowers. The tent was lowered over the bodies and a cairn of snow erected, topped by a cross fashioned from skis.

HIS MOTHER DANCES: I never actually saw my mother dance but I suspect she always harboured a secret urge to do so.

IN GRACE: Dementia is a one of the alarming traps that lie in wait for those of us who grow old and must be a heartbreaking burden for those whose loved ones succumb to it. I like to imagine that the sufferer dwells in an altered but not unhappy world.

A POEM ABOUT LOVE: In a committed relationship, especially one of long-standing, a state of shared dependance develops that can, so easily, be pitched into a state of limbo by the incapacity of one or the other partner.

PICNIC: Some images imprint themselves on our minds at an early age and are never dislodged. One of mine is the tartan rug that used to mark our spot on the beach at Portstewart when we went there for a family picnic. I cannot think of it today without experiencing a Proustian "Madeleine-moment" of pure joy.

AWAKING ADAM: The Creation Story from the Bible is the inspiration for this poem, a celebration of life and the exhilaration of being alive.

STONE WITNESS: For National Poetry Day 2016, a number of British poets were commissioned by BBC Birmingham to write in the imagined voice of an iconic object closely associated with their region of residence. I was one of those selected. My choice was La Gran'mère, an ancient menhir statue much loved by the people of Guernsey.

OCTOBER RAIN: Throughout history, warfare has been a significant driving force behind invention and humans have shown amazing ingenuity when it comes to creating instruments of death.

RECLUSE: Loneliness can occur at any time in one's social development but in old age it can be a source of bitter regret, even self-pity. In an examined life, however, the cause is often found to be attributable to oneself.

LAST MOMENTS: According to T S Eliot, the world ends, not with a bang but with a whimper. I'd sooner imagine it ending in one glorious spasm.

RED UMBRELLA: This rather sinister poem began as a love story, but ended with what is, arguably, the ultimate act of love. It was only on its completion that I noticed a marked similarity to Ros Willard's splendid poem, Con Amore.

ICARUS: The Greek myth of Icarus is a cautionary tale about a youth who, despite warnings, flew too close to the sun. The story inspired many splendid paintings including one by Breughel which features in the celebrated poem by W H Auden, Musee des Beaux Arts.

IMAGES: I'm saddened by how much of life nowadays seems to be experienced on screens of one kind or another and how infrequently we choose to enjoy it hands-on. Rather like Tennyson's Lady of Shalott, we only see reflections of the outside world.

LAMENT: Written immediately after one of the first Islamic terrorist atrocities in Paris, this villanelle is exactly what the title implies, a passionate expression of grief or sorrow.

TURQUOISE SKY: I wrote this poem in 2016, the centenary of the Battle of the Somme, where one million men were wounded or killed, the nature of war changed forever and mass casualties in conflict became the norm.

FUTURE AWAITS: I have a particular favourite among the photographs that still exist of my mother and father. In it, they appear to be quite young and are seated on rocks by an angry sea, possibly the Atlantic. Framed, it graces our hall table.

JUDEN: I learned about the fate of celebrated author, Irene Nemerovsky, when I read the preamble to Suite Francaise, her unfinished novel-sequence written following the German occupation of France during World War Two. Six million Jews, Gypsies and disabled people were murdered in the Nazi death camps at this time.

MEMENTO MORI: All that we hold dear, and much that we take for granted, can so easily be snatched away by an unexpected turn of events. The Latin, Memento Mori translates as, Remember that you must die.

KING OF THE HILL: When I lived in Edinburgh, I heard the eerie tale of Deacon Brodie, a respected public figure by day and a notorious criminal by night. Said to be the inspiration for R L Stevenson's Dr Jekyll and Mr Hyde, his behaviour demonstrated the gulf that often exists in public life between image and reality.

TITANIC: My maternal grandfather, David Crawford, worked in Belfast's Harland and Woolf yard during the building of the world's most famous liner, Titanic. Those of us who hail from that proud shipyard town feel a special affinity with that doomed vessel.

JIHAD: The public are rapidly becoming desensitised to terrorist atrocities and the process is being hastened by the mealy-mouthed vocabulary used by our news-providers. Overnight, it seems, murderous fanatics have become simply 'militants'.

REQUIEM FOR A GAMBLER: My paternal grandfather was an inveterate gambler who experienced the financial highs and inevitable lows that punctuate a gambler's life. There's an old saying in Northern Ireland that the only person who makes money following horses is a ploughman.

ENDGAME: This is a poem about fear: not fear of the unknown but, instead, that mounting terror which one feels as, inevitably, night approaches. I envy those lucky souls whose talismans are sufficient to persuade them that a welcoming light awaits them beyond the darkness.

## About the poem Stone Witness

*A remarkable piece of work, and one that must have given great pleasure to your fellow islanders.*

Michael Swan

*A poem of magnificent sweep and stature, that may just be the single best poem ever written about the island.*

Peter Kenny

*I still tear up when I even think about the poem.*

Jenny Kendall-Tobias

## Other books by this Author

A Guernsey Double (2010) ISBN 978-095660191-9
Strange Journey (2012) ISBN 978-0-9566019-3-3

www.redhandwriter.blogspot.com